WORSHIP THE KING

Old Testament Times and Today

KAREN MALLOY STEVER

PublishAmerica
Baltimore

© 2013 by Karen Malloy Stever.
All rights reserved. No part of this book may be reproduced, stored in a retrieval system or transmitted in any form or by any means without the prior written permission of the publishers, except by a reviewer who may quote brief passages in a review to be printed in a newspaper, magazine or journal.

First printing

PublishAmerica has allowed this work to remain exactly as the author intended, verbatim, without editorial input.

The scripture quotations are taken from the Holman Christian Standard Bible, Copyright 1999, 2000, 2002, 2003 by Holman Bible Publishers. Used by permission.

Softcover 9781630007010
PUBLISHED BY PUBLISHAMERICA, LLLP
www.publishamerica.com
Baltimore

Printed in the United States of America

CONTENTS

About the Photographer/Typist 6
In Loving Memory 9
About the Author 12
Acknowledgements 15
INTRODUCTION 16
Psalm 100 17
Psalm 150 19
The Harp and the Lyre 22
His Light is Love 24
Israelis-Music During Time of Old Testament 27
Modern Day Praise and Worship 32
Music and Prayer are Anointed by Christ 34
Jesus is the Light of the World for all Nations 37
Psalm 98, Praise the King 38
Jesus is the Good Shepherd Abiding in the Field 40
Keep Your Eye on the Sparrow 41
The Beatitudes 43
Reveal Yourself to me Lord 45
Let Us Come Rejoicing 47
Psalm 149 49
Prince of Peace 51
Choirs of Angels Rejoicing 53
Psalm 148, Creations Praise of the Lord 56
Other Books Published by Author, Karen Malloy Stever 58

4   Karen Malloy Stever

DEDICATION

This book is dedicated to God and His son, Jesus Christ, to whom we give all glory, honor, and praise. All worship leaders, singers, musicians, and prayer warriors who love and serve the Lord, continue to lift up your hands to the holy one. Exalt his name before all people. Give God the praise and adoration that is due him.

Sing and dance before your Lord and Savior, Jesus Christ. Wave banners and glorify His name! Glory to God in the highest.

About the Photographer/Typist

Teresa Willette serves the Lord through her daily ministry working with children and youth who enter into the treatment foster care system. She enjoys creating families and successful lives for God's children. Ms. Willette enjoys helping others for the glory of God's kingdom.

Ms. Willette has her Master's degree in Counseling and Psychology and is from Puerto Rico. Ms. Willette was adopted as a baby and this is what led her to advocate for those who aren't able to do so on their own.

Ms. Willette appreciates the thoughtful and awesome opportunity that God gave her to be a part of assisting Ms. Stever with the successful creation and publication of her Christian books. To God be all the glory, honor, and adoration!

"Teresa Willette, God's faithful servant"

"Daniel Malloy, Celia Sacco-Wedding 1947"

In Loving Memory

With a grateful heart in remembrance of my mother, Celia Sacco Malloy, of Utica and Clinton, New York, who passed away on Thursday of Easter week, April 5, 2012. Mom encouraged and inspired my brothers Daniel, Robin, Eric, and Gary and my sister Dana and I to use our gifts and talents to express our faith and beliefs. We love and miss you Mom. Find comfort in the loving arms of Jesus, your Savior.

Your daughter,
Karen

Celia Malloy with children and grandchildren.

Author Karen Malloy Stever

About the Author

Author, Karen Malloy Stever was born in New York. She graduated from Canton College in upstate New York. Ms. Stever worked at the State Department in Washington D.C. and substitute taught in Virginia schools and in the Department of Defense schools overseas. Ms. Stever and family lived at the American Embassy in Bonn, Germany for several years. Ms. Stever served on missionary teams in Nigeria, West Africa, Albania in Eastern Europe. She spent time in the Holy Land and studied theology with the Bible Institute of Liberty University.

Ms. Stever served as Minister of Music, Choir Director, and Soloist at various churches in Virginia. Currently she is in the process of publishing eight books under religion area and children's story books. Ms. Stever is also involved in evangelistic and missionary work. One of her current projects is gathering shoes, sandals and sneakers to send to the children in India and Nepal. Ms. Stever is also involved in prayer and healing ministry and sponsors children in India, and Nepal. She supports the good works of "World Vision" and "Mission of Mercy" worldwide, now called "One Child Matters".

Ms. Stever has two daughters, Teresa and husband, Michael Penn of Virginia, and two grandchildren, Korsen and Kaela Penn. Her daughter Maryann Stever lives in South Carolina.

KAREN STEVER WITH GRANDCHILDREN,
KAELA AND KORSEN PENN, VA

Acknowledgements

I thank God, his son, Jesus Christ, and the Holy Spirit, for all of the love and inspiration they have given me to write this book.

I would also like to thank my daughter, Teresa Penn, for all her hard work typing two of my books late at night and for all her support and love.

I want to thank my daughter, Maryann Stever, for all her love and encouragement along the way.

I wish to thank my very good friend, Teresa Willette, for all her hard work typing and re-typing several of my books and continuous email correspondence with the publishing company. I thank Ms. Willette for all her love, kindness, and support. I love you all dearly.

INTRODUCTION

People among the nations speak many different languages and have diverse cultures. Jesus walks among his people and anoints his chosen vessels and sends them out to the nations. He is very pleased with the magnificent praise and worship the people give to him. Jesus knows all, hears all, and sees all things. He continues to pour out blessings and gifts of the holy spirit upon his children.

Jesus is alive and moves among his people. He is happy with the worship that choir members, praise teams, bands, and congregations present to him each week during services. The spirit of the Lord resides within the hearts of God's people. You will feel God's peace, love, mercy, and forgiving heart as you come into his presence.

Jesus wishes for us to love him with our whole heart, mind, body, and soul. Jesus spoke to the Samaritan woman in John 4:23-24 "True worshippers will worship the father in spirit, and those who worship him must worship in spirit and truth." Jesus requires us to love and walk humbly with our God.

Psalm 100

Shout triumphantly to the Lord, all the earth.

Serve the Lord with gladness,

Come before Him with joyful songs.

Acknowledge that the Lord is God.

He made us and we are His,

His people, the sheep of His pasture.

Enter His gates with thanksgiving

And his courts with praise!

Give thanks to Him and praise His name.

For the Lord is good, and His love is eternal,

His faithfulness endures through all generations.

CELIA MALLOY AND GRANDCHILDREN, GINA CLAXTON
AND GIOVANNI MALLOY, SYRACUSE, NY.

Psalm 150

Hallelujah!

Praise God in His sanctuary

Praise Him in His mighty heavens

Praise Him for His powerful acts;

Praise Him for His abundant greatness

Praise Him with trumpet blast

Praise Him with harp and lyre

Praise Him with tambourines and dance

Praise Him with flute and strings

Praise Him with resounding cymbals

Praise Him with clashing cymbals

Let everything that breathes praise the Lord.
                        Hallelujah!

JUNIOR CELEBRATION SINGERS

WORSHIP

The Harp and the Lyre

With music and dancing

The harp and lyre

Give glory to the King of Kings

May the anthems ring out

With screams and shouts

In jubilation lift up your voices and sing

With hearts full of passion

May his name be exalted

Give adoration to the King of Kings

May his name live forever

Jehovah Shalom is his peace

With joy, happiness, and glory it brings.

Author: Karen Malloy Stever

Worship The King 23

JESUS HEALING THE SICK

His Light is Love

Let all receive the love of God
That is ours to enjoy each day

Big or small, tall or short
It has no limits to say

It's reachable and attainable
Lift up your hearts and pray

Receive the gift
Wrapped in blessing and grace
Pure holiness in a light of praise

With praying hands and shouts of joy
Be seated by the King of Kings

His name is Jesus

His light is love

For all eternity, let the children sing

To a world that is lost

He paid the cost

He rose to heaven on the angel's wing

Hallelujah!

Author: Karen Malloy Stever

CRUCIFICTION OF JESUS CHRIST, JERUSALEM

Israelis-Music During Time of Old Testament

Israelis long ago and today have always enjoyed music, singing, and dancing as forms of praise and worship to their God, Yahweh. When welcoming soldiers home from battle, dancers were accompanied by song and instruments in 1 Samuel 18:6. The workers bringing in the harvest might sing a song, Isaiah 16:10, Jeremiah 48:33. In ancient Israel, music and dance were performed in their religious and secular lives.

In Genesis 4:21, music is mentioned for the first time. Lamech's son, Jubal, brought music to their Hebrew culture. Some workers used chants like Numbers 21:17-18. Some singing and dancing brought condemnation such as the golden calf in Exodus 32:17-19, which symbolized a broken covenant. The Song of Miriam, one of the oldest poetic verses in the Old Testament, celebrated victory over Pharaoh in Exodus 15:21. Judges 5 is a musical witness to Israel's victory over Jabin.

This was the "Song of Deborah." Samson had musical chants after he slayed the Philistines in Judges 15:16. When David was courageous in battle, women sang, "Saul has slain his thousands and David his ten thousands" 1 Samuel 18:7.

Psalm 98 says:

Shout to the Lord, all the earth,

Be jubilant, shout for joy and sing.

Sing to the Lord with the lyre.

With the lyre and melodious song.

With trumpets and blast of ram's horn

Shout triumphantly in the presence of the

Lord, our King.

Worship in the Old Testament also featured the trumpet sounds in Numbers 10:10, and songs of thanksgiving and praise in 2 Chronicles 29:20-30. The structure in some Psalms shows vocal singing of refrains such as "Lift up your heads, O gates, rise up ancient doors in Psalm 24 and Hallelujah.

Psalm is applied to 57 songs in the Bible. The psalter refers to songs with just instruments. Almost fifty nine Psalms start their heading with "to the choir master." Psalm 4, 6, 54 include stringed instruments.

A very popular instrument in the Bible is the "shofar" or ram's horn. It plays up to three notes. It was used as a trumpet in times of peace and war, Judges 3:27, 6:34, Nehemiah 4:18-20. The shofar would announce new moons, Sabbaths, and gave warnings when the people were in danger. It is still used in the synagogue today. It has an important place in the life of Israel. It is used in national celebrations, 1 Kings 1:34, 2 Kings 9:13.

The trumpet was the instrument of the priests, Numbers 10:2-10. The trumpet introduced temple ceremony and sacrifice, 2 Kings 12:13, Numbers 31:6. David played the lyre and the harp, Isaiah 23:16, 2 Samuel 6:5. The harp was also a favorite instrument of the Egyptians. Other instruments mentioned in the Bible were flutes, pipes, woodwinds, tambourines, cymbals, and bells. During the Babylonian exile, the Hebrews sang the Lord's song in Psalm 37. They established the temple and had decadents of the Levitical musicians, Ezra 2:40-41, gain responsibility for the Liturgical music. Song and dance is very much a part of Israel. Their culture, praise and worship continue today.

CELEBRATION SINGERS

DIRECTOR, KAREN MALLOY STEVER

WOODBRIDGE, VA

Modern Day Praise and Worship

Churches today across the United States use different formats for praise and worship. Traditional services tend to use instruments such as organs, pianos, violins, flutes, drums, clarinets, guitars, and trumpets. Usually the older hymns sung are very familiar to the congregation such as, "Amazing Grace", "Onward Christian Soldiers", "How Great Thou Art" and "Blessed Assurance."

Some churches have a folk or gospel music service. To reach the middle to younger groups, there is also the contemporary service using a variety of instruments such as flutes, maracas, tambourines, conga drums, drums, acoustic and bass guitars, pianos, organs, keyboards, trumpets, trombones and clarinets.

It is common today to see various types of choirs, praise teams, and soloists singing a variety of music to please all people. Southern gospel, black gospel, and contemporary music is diversified in different languages with various beat and rhythm patterns.

Much of the modern contemporary music is high energy level, fast pace, joyful and uplifting. Many of the songs originate with the Christian recording artists of today that we hear on the radio and in concert.

Other forms of worship include puppet ministry, skits, human video, which allow free expression. Worship also includes prayers, poetry, drama, and singing. The focus for all worship is our God the Father, Jesus His son, and the Holy Spirit. Worship is an expression of our praise, honor, and love for a higher being and power which is Yahweh, Jehovah, our God, and Creator.

May your worship of the King of Kings and Lord of Lords increase and have a deeper meaning in your life, as you continue to develop a relationship with your Abba Father, The Good Shepherd, the Creator of the universe.

Music and Prayer are Anointed by Christ

Song, dance, music, and prayer are holy and anointed by Christ. People worship their Lord and Savior and lift up holy hands. They cry and weep for who he is. Musicians, singers, dancers, and prayer warriors are Christ's chosen vessels he will use to save the world. Worshippers raise banners in his name. People and children sing and dance before the King of Kings and Lord of Lords. Their loving spirit is poured out into the sanctuary.

Jesus is a living sacrifice for all mankind. Feel his presence, love, and mercy during your praise, worship and prayer time. He is your healing stream that runs through the sanctuary. Receive healing today and be set free by the power of Jesus Christ. He is your Abba Father, so accept all the love he has for you. He will bathe you in the light of his forgiveness.

Jesus calls each of you by name. He is your peace when there is no peace and your joy when there is no joy. He is your hope when there is no hope. Jesus is the truth, the way, and the light. Come unto him and he will give you rest. Step into God's presence as his spirit resides there in a beautiful way. Jesus holds the key to your salvation. He will unlock the door to your heart during praise, worship, and prayer time.

Pray, laugh, cry, lift up holy hands, bow and kneel before your King. Jesus is the King of Glory now and for all eternity. He loves you all very dearly. He wishes to set you apart and make you holy. God wants to bestow blessings and graces upon you. He is Jehovah. Give him all the honor and praise that is due him.

PRAYER

Jesus is the Light of the World for all Nations

Jesus is the light of the world for all nations, tribes, and tongues. Let Jesus shed his light of glory upon you. His light and heart penetrate through all mankind. Jesus wants to save and rescue his beloved people. Then, all will be calm, peaceful, and joyful in his presence. All people one day will bow beneath his feet and recognize him as the Messiah, Savior of the world. His name will be exalted as King of Kings and Lord of Lords.

Jesus is the Son of the living God, and his kingdom shall have no end. He is Alpha and Omega, beginning and end of all things. Jesus is the flame that lights the whole world. His glory and majesty shine across the whole earth and fill the heavens.

Psalm 98
Praise the King

Sing a new song to the Lord

For He has performed wonders;

His right hand and holy arm

have won Him victory.

The Lord has made his victory known;

He has revealed His righteousness

in the sight of the nations.

He has remembered His love

and faithfulness to the house of Israel;

all the needs of the earth

have seen our God's victory.

Shout to the Lord, all the earth;

Be jubilant; shout for joy and sing,

Sing to the Lord with the lyre,

With the lyre and melodious song.

With trumpets and blast of ram's horn

shout triumphantly

in the presence of the Lord, our King.

Let the sea and all that fills it

the world and those who live in it, resound.

Let the rivers clap their hands;

Let the mountains shout

together for joy before the Lord,

For He is coming to judge the earth.

He will judge the world righteously

And the people fairly.

Jesus is the Good Shepherd Abiding in the Field

Jesus is the Good Shepherd abiding in the field and he holds a precious lamb. He longs to hold you close to him. Humble yourselves before the sight of the Lord, your Savior. Give God your praise, worship, and adoration. Bow before the foot of the cross and repent of your sins. Jesus will show you mercy, kindness, and forgiveness. He wishes to change your heart and capture it for himself. He is the Good Shepherd and wants to set you free and wipe away every tear from your eyes. Step into the healing stream, the living waters of Christ's loving kindness and receive salvation and the right to enter eternal glory, heaven with your Lord and Savior.

Keep Your Eye on the Sparrow

Precious heart of Jesus hear my humble prayer today. I surrender all that I am and all that I have to you. Make me an instrument of your peace. Help me extend your love and mercy to all mankind. Use me to save souls for the kingdom of God. Purify my heart and make it worthy to receive grace and blessings. Let your heart dwell within mine. May your holy light shine through me always.

Karen Malloy Stever

THE CHURCH OF THE BEATITUDES, ISRAEL

The Beatitudes

In Matthew 4:19 Jesus said, "Follow me and I will make you fishers of men." Jesus was teaching and preaching the good news throughout Galilee, Jerusalem, Judea, and beyond Jordan. He healed many that were afflicted with disease, epilepsy, and demon possession. When Jesus encountered large crowds, he walked up the mountain and gathered his disciples and taught them: The Beatitudes.

Blessed are the poor in spirit,

because the kingdom of heaven is theirs.

Blessed are those who mourn,

because they will be comforted.

Blessed are the gentle,

because they will inherit the earth.

Blessed are those who hunger

and thirst for righteousness,

because they will be filled.

Blessed are the merciful,

because they will be shown mercy.

Blessed are the pure in heart,

because they will see God.

Blessed are the peacemakers,

because they will be called sons of God.

Blessed are those who are persecuted for righteousness,

because the kingdom of heaven is theirs.

Blessed are you when they insult you and persecute you,

and falsely say every kind of evil against you because of me.

Be glad and rejoice, because your reward is great in heaven,

For that is how they persecuted the prophets who were before you.

Reveal Yourself to me Lord

Lord, in my times of weakness, please come to me. Surround me and enfold me in your loving arms and show me the right path to follow. I long to hear your voice and commune with you. If only I could feel your presence. Dear Lord, talk to me, answer my questions and be my friend. I love you and need you. I call out to you in the midst of sin and darkness. Save me from the snares of the devil. In you Lord, lay all holiness, purity, goodness, and hope. Help me save myself before it is too late. Do not let my soul perish. Redeem me Lord because I love you very much.

Use me Lord and set me apart. Let me be a light in a dark, sinful world. Plant a seed of love and forgiveness in me, Lord. Use me to reach the nations. Send me out to preach the gospel message of your great love, mercy, loving kindness, and forgiveness to all people. Help me imitate you Lord. May I learn to forgive my enemies and not judge others. May I be slow to anger and always stress reconciliation and healing. Lord, help me to see the sanctity and holiness of all human life from the time of conception until the natural death of a person. You are the giver of life and you take away life. It is precious and sacred in the eyes of our Creator.

Let Us Come Rejoicing

May the Son of God, Jesus Christ, shine His face upon us this day and may we glory in his presence. Pray that the risen Lord will reside in our hearts. Jesus is our comforter in times of sorrow, pain, and tears. Call upon the name of Jesus and he will carry us through the valley of tears and we will come out rejoicing in his love and mercy. Jesus, your heart of grace fills us to overflowing and frees us from earthly suffering. Our kingdom is not of this world. In heaven, we will attain immense joy and happiness that surpasses all understanding.

Jesus holds the key to our salvation. Unlock the door to my heart Lord and abide in me today. Show me the path to follow that will lead to your eternal throne in heaven. I long to live and dwell with you in total peace, joy, love, and harmony for all eternity.

EASTER PRODUCTION

CHRIST CHAPEL, WOODBRIDGE, VA

Psalm 149

Praise for God's triumph,

Halleluiah!

Sing to the Lord a new song,

His praise in the assembly of the godly.

Let Israel celebrate its maker,

Let the children of Zion rejoice in their king.

Let them praise His name with dancing,

and make music to Him with tambourine and lyre.

For the Lord takes pleasure in His people,

He adorns the humble with salvation.

Let the godly celebrate in triumphant glory!

Let them shout for joy on their beds.

Let the exaltation of God be in their mouths

and a two edged sword in their hands,

inflicting vengeance on the nations

and punishment on the peoples,

binding their kings with chains,

and their dignitaries with iron shackles,

carrying out the judgment decreed against them.

This honor is for all His godly people.

Hallelujah!

Prince of Peace

In a manger lay a baby born

To save the world from shame and scorn

We gaze upon our Savior's face

Extend our arms for a warm embrace

He came to set the captives free

To release the world of poverty

His light shines down through all the earth

The miracle of life, baby Jesus birth

Let's give thanks to the father above

He sent His son for us to love

In a Bethlehem manger long ago

Were many stars all aglow

Let the angels proclaim His heavenly birth

Give glory in the highest

to the Prince of peace on earth.

Author: Karen Malloy Stever

Choirs of Angels Rejoicing

My heart fills up with devotion
When I enter the gate of your home

Choirs of angels rejoicing
Sit at the feet of your throne

Shouts with clapping and jubilation
Swell up in our hearts today

For we've come to rejoice
Yes we've come to rejoice

In your presence
We pray this day

Sing halleluiah, praise Jehovah
We will bow down at your feet
Sing halleluiah, praise Jehovah
May our life in you be complete

At the table we lay out a banquet
As we join in a feast with our Lord

All the choirs of angels rejoicing
With the mighty strength of our swords

Shouts with clapping and jubilation
Swell up in our hearts today

As we give you the praise
And our banners we'll raise
As we dwell in your heart today

Sing halleluiah, praise Jehovah
We will bow down at your feet

Sing halleluiah, praise Jehovah
May our life in you be complete.

Author: Karen Malloy Stever

Psalm 148
Creations Praise of the Lord

Halleluiah!

Praise the Lord from the heavens;

Praise Him in the heights.

Praise Him, all His angels;

Praise Him, all His hosts.

Praise Him sun and moon;

Praise Him, all you shining stars.

Praise Him, highest heavens,

And you waters above the heavens.

Let them praise the name of the Lord,

for He commanded, and they were created.

He set them in position forever and ever,

He gave an order that will never pass away.

Praise the Lord from the earth,

All sea monsters and ocean depths,

lightning and hail, snow and cloud,

powerful wind that executes His command,

mountains and all hills,

fruit trees and all cedars,

wild animals and all cattle,

creatures that crawl and flying birds,

Kings of the earth and all peoples,

Princes and all judges of the earth,

Young man as well as young woman,

old and young together.

Let them praise the name of the Lord,

for His name alone is exalted.

His majesty covers heaven and earth.

He has raised up a horn for his people,

praise from all His godly ones,

from the Israelites, the people close to Him.

Halleluiah!

Other Books Published by Author, Karen Malloy Stever

1. Jesus Manifests His Glory
2. Jabin The Talking Donkey In Jerusalem, Children's' book
3. Rosa The Lost Lamb-Village in Albania

Click on Amazon.com to order books by this author.